COME INTO MY GARDEN

Volume 1

Their young romance was deliberately put asunder by a grandmother who had her own plans for whom her granddaughter should marry. All contact was lost for 58 years, but the fires of love have rekindled. The author, Virgil Ballard, has been inspired to express his feelings in poetry. This collection of poems range from tear evoking sadness to joy and elation and even the nonsensical. There are emotions expressed here that everyone can empathize with. Easy to read; hard to put down.

By Virgil Ballard

Order this book online at www.trafford.com
or email orders@trafford.com

Most Trafford titles are also available at major online book retailers.

Printed in Victoria, BC, Canada.

ISBN: 978-1-4269-2825-3 (sc)

*Our mission is to efficiently provide the world's finest, most comprehensive book publishing
service, enabling every author to experience success. To find out how to publish your book, your
way, and have it available worldwide, visit us online at www.trafford.com*

Trafford rev. 5/13/2010

 www.trafford.com

North America & international
toll-free: 1 888 232 4444 (USA & Canada)
phone: 250 383 6864 ♦ fax: 812 355 4082

Contents

To Ruth, Who Above All, Inspired Me To Write This Poetry.

Mail Call

I stood in back at mail call
Hoping they might call my name
Other men opened their letters
But for me it was always the same
I tried to hide my feelings
As I shrugged and turned away
I was too macho to show I cared
But the hurt was there to stay
They say hope springs eternal
And I know that to be true
Even when you know its over
And hoping makes you blue
Years passed slowly, 20,40, 50 and more
One day I got a letter though
With her name, there in the corner
As I held it, my old hands trembled so
Then casting my eyes upward
A prayer was in my heart
So bitter sweet my feelings
So many long years apart
Ever so slowly I opened it
Though I could barely see
Tears blurred my eyesight
No longer the macho me
First I turned it over
She signed it "love" I saw
All reason quickly left me
Old defenses began to thaw
Now I'm sure the people wonder
Why I have a secret smile
God laid his hand upon me
I can call her mine for awhile

The Silver Chord

Remember when you loved me
Before our plans went awry
Remembering when you loved me
Always makes me cry

For many years another held you
I wish it could have been me
You've built a lifetime of memories with another
And with another raised a family

Why do I continue this torture?
Why can't I just let it go
Because the silver chord was never broken
We're still connected, that I know

I know your life has been happy
And perhaps it's just as well
That you never shared my heartaches
Never knew the road to hell

But if your life should ever change
Have a look over your shoulder I'll be waiting in the shadows
The same boy only much older

The Damn Alarm

Her wings were transparent
Like made of cellophane
I heard her tapping as she hovered
Just outside my window pane

She was so very tiny
As fairies are wont to be
She said she had a message
A message just for me

I opened the window and
She lit upon my hand
She was dressed like a princess
It all seemed so grand

She was quite impatient
As she tapped her tiny toe
She said cupid had sent her
And I really aught to go

That my lover had summoned
To meet in a secret spot
She was there to guide me
In case I had forgot

Of course I consented
And she raised her little wand
Then the alarm sounded
Before she could respond

Just An Old Woman

The old woman sat with a shawl on her lap
Eagerly watching every one passing by
She was tied in her chair with a big cotton strap
Watching her, it was hard to keep your eyes dry

The nurses were all busy going to and fro
If any one came close, she reached out to touch
Hoping to talk and always asking to know
Reaching with bony fingers hoping to clutch

Always the same question with a pleading smile
"Can you please take me home?"
She was so frail, so determined all the while
If any one would listen,"can you please take me home?"

With snow white hair done up in a bun
She was probably a beauty back in her day
Had she no family? Was there no one?
How long must she ask? How long must she stay?

Her days must pass slowly always asking to go
There is probably only one way she will ever leave
Her hope is a blessing because she doesn't know
And when she is gone no one will grieve

The Strangest Story

This is the strangest story that I have to tell
If you can't believe it
Its probably just as well
Lest I forget and cant retrieve it

Here's what happened late one night
As I lay in my bed all alone
My room was bathed in dim moonlight
My longing had a power of its own

Ah the strength when two loves combine
It has a force only God can do
It warped the matrix of space and time
And in an instant pulled her through

Imagining her there seemed so real
My yearning had never been this strong
Her body warmth I could actually feel
I was wide awake, don't get me wrong

And as I looked I could see her form
Then she stirred and turned to me
Her breath on my face felt so warm
Twas not a dream but reality

We made love all night you see
We hugged and kissed and held on tight
We gave no thought how this could be
We just knew it felt so right

I dozed off ere mornings dawn
So content in her warm embrace
When I awoke, I found her gone
The smell of sex had left its trace

Yes time and space again had closed
She's back home in another state
If only I'd held on tighter, instead I dozed
But wishful thinking is now too late

And when we talked a few hours hence
"you'd never guess my dream," she said
She couldn't keep me in suspense
"1 dreamed that I was in your bed"

A Little White House

That little white house still stands
Built ever so carefully with loving hands
A beautiful setting back against the hill
He persevered by strength of will
Carefully selecting each board and nail
He put them together with loving detail
They say he built it for his bride-to-be
Expecting it to be home for he and she
He carefully tended this pretty little home
He was often seen there but always alone
He cleaned and repainted as the years wore on
Pruning the roses and trimming the lawn
He grew old and stooped and became lame
But he was ready for the bride who never came
Many years later this story is told
About this old man who became too old
One summer evening as it was getting late
A frail old lady appeared at the gate
She stood for awhile, then climbed the hill
To a little white cross that stands there still
A strange thing happened as darkness fell
And this is the story they always tell
In the old house, empty and dark, appeared a light
Seen through a window far into the night
Then the old rose bushes long thought dead
Suddenly came to life with blossoms of red
That strange old lady left without a trace
Tho rumor has it that it was her place
That little white house is still never lived in
Almost as a symbol of what might have been

The Matriarch

There are four generations in her down line
Beautiful women and girls all mighty fine
She can be proud of the job she has done
They have dignity and class every one

No better tribute will one ever need
Than to have your offspring follow your lead
Mother, grandmother and great grandma
She's certainly the best that they ever saw

This matriarch is a super neat lady
Working every day as she approaches eighty
She is very familiar with hard work and strife
But there's a really weird twist in her secret life

There's a man in the shadows, weathered and worn
He's been there even before the firstborn
It s their secret; no one must know
She is his girl and he is her beau

Can you imagine hot lovers old and gray
This secret will die with them one day
It was all in their dreams, certainly, of course
If you hear differently, consider the source

The Sequel

`Twas "Dream Catcher' that made them famous
The sequel is by far the best
Tho it was the love story of the ages
There is a mystery needs put to rest
That empty grave leaves an untold story
Whatever happened to forbidden fruit
Where is the gravesite of pretty Ruth
After years of searching, no records can be found
Did Virg and Ruth ever get together
Many rumors do abound
A rather strange phenomenon has come to pass
The descendants of the Ballards and the Saunders
No kinship by blood, which is the truth
They have an annual family reunion
To celebrate the story of Virg and of Ruth
Another persistent rumor that just won't go away
And we know there could be no hanky panky
Where official records are concerned
Tho state archivists are often very cranky
Any faulty records would surely get them burned
The rumor says if Virg should be exhumed
Quite a surprised just might be found
Not one but two skeletons there lie entwined
Since they couldn't get together while living it's assumed
By golly they managed somehow six feet underground

Comfortable

Our love is comfortable like an old shoe
No need to pretend or watch what we say
We know each other tho it all seems so new
And we like what we have and know it's okay

We¹ re not enamored by show and by glitz
We like ourselves and who we are
So we like each other, that's as simple as it gets
Our love is fulfilled even from afar

The Second Phase

Many many years with loving care
She has curled and cut and washed their hair
She's counseled many with sage advice
And listens by the hour for the same low price

She hears their stories of family and friends
Making sure their hair has no loose ends
They're her ladies and she loves them all
She's a bundle of joy but not very tall

They used to be many but now are few
She's always there for the last hair-do
When its their time to be laid to rest
She donates her time so they look their best

She's nearing the time when this job is through
This vibrant lady has better things to do
Always helping others has really been great
Now it's her turn before it's too late

There's so much to life for her yet to live
Let others come forth, it's their turn to give
To assume the burden of getting things done
Tho many may offer, I hope I'm the one

She can dress in fine linens & sleep late each day
She'll be pampered and spoiled, breakfast on a tray
No busy schedule that she'll have to keep
This lady has sowed, now she can reap

She needs to laugh and dance each day
No more worries about bills to pay
Happily singing for all to see
She can throw up her hands and say "I'M FREE"

The Yearning

There is a feeling getting stronger
And stronger by the hour
As the hours stretch into days
And the days fill up the weeks
The weeks add up to months
And the months consume my tears

Its not just a gentle tugging
That pulls my heart apart
Its an all consuming yearning
To have you near and touching
To look deep into your eyes
And to know your very soul

Just to put my arms around you
And press your body close
To hold you ever closer
And never never let you go
I would cover you with kisses
From your head down to your toes

I long to tell you of my wishes
Tho we know it cannot be
If you see me from a distance
With a sort of wistful smile
Give me a knowing wink
It may help me for awhile

Grandpa

He sat upon the old weathered stump
Obviously thinking as he whittled
Some might think him just a grump
But his acuity should not be belittled

His eyes twinkled with a real sense of humor
A wrinkled old face foretold his years
The wisdom here alleged was not just rumor
He had earned the respect of all of his peers

Grandpa is what I called him back then
I was intimidated with respect and awe
He was the example of what to expect of men
One of the most honorable men I ever saw

An Old Man

I saw an old man staring at me
He looked sorta familiar in a way
I was looking back in time I could see
He had come from the past just arriving today

The lines on his face were not grim
In fact they hinted at frequent smiles
His eyes told me life had not always favored him
As he traversed the weary years and miles

Since he was staring, I stared at him too
I lifted my hand as if to wave
He did the same as if he knew
Then we smiled and I continued to shave

I'd like to know that old man better
We seem to be somewhat alike
We've even chosen to wear the same sweater
I feel like I've known him since I was a tyke

Prayers

As I listen to their prayers
In many different lands and creeds
It matters not what is my name
What matters is the total of their deeds

Some chant by memory and by rote
With no thought to what they say
Many requests have a selfish note
Many know not how to pray

Some have loved ones in dire need
Some seek relief from daily strife
Some cry my name aloud, indeed
With scant moments left of life

Some are silent and some are loud
Some alone and many in a crowd
Some are meek and some are proud
Some look upward and some are bowed

If you really want to find the way
Have compassion for your fellow man
There is no secret way to pray
Just spread your love as best you can

Please know this while yet you live
What ere your status in life may be
You always receive in proportion to what you give
I know this because I am WE

The Letters Stopped

"I love you, dear, and I always will"
Then all words stopped as if each had died
Had something evil swooped in for the kill
Not another word passed though long they tried

In time each gave up and blamed the other
Assuming they had each found another
"I love you, dear, and I always will"
Were the last words ever written until

Sixty years of their lives had slowly passed
One day they met face to face at last
Both old and gray and married, of course
They compared notes to determine the source

Of all bizarre things that can't be topped
Someone kept stealing their mail til the letters stopped
Too late now to undo that vicious deed
They still feel the same but no way to proceed

A Cow And Her Calf

There is an old cow I know
That has a runty calf
He's always behind and very slow
Only as big as others his age by half

But this old cow is proud of him
Just as proud as if he was a good one
His chances of being a good beef are none and slim
But that old cow claims him as her son

So if there is a moral to this story
It's that value is in the eyes of the beholder
Some may never achieve fame and glory
Let us extend to all a warm shoulder

My Extra-Ordinary Ordinary Girl

There is no pretense anywhere about her
She never tries to be what she is not
This ordinary girl to which I refer
Has no clue to all that she has got

She's so humble in her perfection
She has every thing a man could desire
Plus I'm the recipient of her affection
All she is and has I do admire

In any string there is always the choicest pearl
One always has the brightest shine
I call her my extra-ordinary ordinary girl
1 am so honored to think of her as mine

A regal beauty that no one can compare
Cheery and bright, she's such a delight
Turning heads as she passes everywhere
She knows not how much she can excite

Walking beside her makes me so proud
Holding her hand makes my body tingle
Thus you see me walking on a cloud
But, alas, this angel is not single

The Outdoor Man

There is an old man I see every day
Always dining alone at the old cafe
His cheeks are ruddy, his hair is gray
He's an outdoor man and walks that way

If anyone happens to catch his eye
He'll smile and nod kinda shy
He'll sit holding his coffee 'til it's cold
Lost in thought of days of old

I wonder, is there anyone in his life
It's pretty obvious there is no wife
I'm sure he must have a story to tell
Is God punishing him? Is this his hell?

I hope his future will see a change
He is no longer out on the range
At time I see his eyes blur with a tear
If there is anyone close, they should be here

An Old Belt Buckle

It was just an old buckle and belt
That a cowboy wore some 50 odd years
When he learned how his woman had felt
It became hers as her birthday nears

Tho he'd worn it many years in the dust and the sun
Riding and branding and working with hay
He rode horses that were ornery as a son-of-a-gun
And some were as gentle as flowers in may

Now his lady is having this belt trimmed down
She'll wear it proudly around her small waist
She'll wear it with honor as a queen wears a crown
To remind her of him and how fast time has raced

Of course the old buckle is shiny and worn
But it means more to her than if it was new
It's a symbol of love long ago torn
A love in spite of all odds has blossomed anew

So if you see a young woman walking proudly in jeans
You'll know there is an old cowboy sorta hidden away
If you ask about her belt and just what it means
She'll tell you it's magic and she'll prove it someday

A Cowboy On Her Mind

She has had a cowboy on her mind
Ever since she was a teen
Only one, she's not the roving kind
But her wants were clear and keen

Tho very young in years, I'm guessing
She had all the needs of a woman
Life has dealt her a mixed blessing
Each time she heads east, it's an omen

A sign that she's leaving and going away
Leaving behind her own lifes fulfillment
Her destiny was stolen from her this way
Now only frustration with never contentment

Sixty years she searched for the cowboy she lost
Fully occupied as a mother and wife
With a successful career but what was the cost
The cost was the loss of romance in her life

Now she has found him, oh what joy
But there is still a chasm they cannot cross
She still cannot have that old cowboy
Is her reward to be "close but still a loss?"

Few will ever know of her sacrifice
Faithful to her duty, true to the end
Something for herself would have been nice
Lucky is he who can call her friend

Dad's Secret

It's sad duty going through dads stuff
Deciding what to keep and what to toss is tough
But I've found something that has made me cry
I had no idea; I never wanted to pry

I guess he was making plans until the last
He left no instructions and I was aghast
Many years a bachelor ,he had never given up
He was still hoping til the last drop in his cup

I found a file labeled "honeymoon account"
Poor dad finally met a hurdle he could not surmount
The file had well worn pictures of an ocean cruise
And several thousand dollars which they planned to use

What Has Happened To Men?

Things you no longer see a man do
Pull out his knife and whittle on a stick
Or even whet his knife on his boot or shoe
Or when needed , sharpen his own toothpick

Men used to meet and squat on their heels
It was a comfortable way to talk a spell
I think modern man doesn't know how it feels
And probably can't even squat very well

Men used to consider women in a special class
They would open doors and hold their coat and chairs
Now days men are often very crass
As with a shrug, so what, who cares

Men never wore earrings, necklaces and worse
I hate shaking a hand soft and fair
Especially if he has a belly pack or purse
Or sports a head of long curly hair

Real men really like women I've found
But they also enjoy the company of men
Pity the poor youth raised with only women around
It's bad for a young male when there is too much estrogen

Pretend

There is a force that's pulling me back
Try as I may, I can't break away
From old memories when they attack
And that old sadness I pray from a long ago day

When I lost, and another you wed
It's a wound that won't heal
So often it's bled as decades have sped
A spirit can be broken when love is so real

I know we must think life is now good
What we now have is the healing salve
For old wounds when understood
Of course you are right, I'll put the past out of sight

I'll carry on with a smile
Having you is great even tho it is late
You are making life so worthwhile
The past was just fate so I'll "pretend" you're my mate

Is It A Deadend?

I know a man who is following a dead end road
I told him once," Sir this road goes nowhere"
He answered," Yes I know; of that I'm well aware
But I can't turn around with this heavy load

Besides I always hope just over the next hill
I'll find a turn that leads to greener grass
No matter the difficulties I may have to pass
I know there is a place where the grass is greener still"

This old man trudges slowly as the world speeds on by
Perhaps he may never achieve his long sought prize
But he's eager to continue his trek at each sunrise
I think he's probably foolish ; why does he even try

I dare not tell him that his quest is a hopeless case
Of course he wouldn't believe it and would just smile
So why disillusion him, he seems happy for awhile
A wise man once said,"The thrill of conquest is in the chase"

Wouldn't it be a strange twist to his lonely case
If it turns out he knows something that I don't
If he wins by perseverance, cause quitting he just won't
Then I'd be the foolish one with egg upon my face

As for the heavy load that he always bore
It was old memories that he couldn't put aside
About a girl that he had hoped to make his bride
Once he completely lost her, now she's standing at his door

In case you're wondering why he doesn't invite her in
She has some heavy baggage that really holds her back
Even with both of them pulling, they cannot get some slack
The end of the story may just be; it might have been

A Long Long Trail

Close your eyes and hear me tell
Of an ancient love that never fell
Sixty years their chance seemed doomed
When out of the dust a flower bloomed
Sixty years with no contact ever made
Who would believe their love refused to fade
She was a beautiful girl full of charm
He a quiet boy right off the farm
A perfect match everyone could tell
'till the old woman from the north cast a spell
Then their connection was torn asunder
With flashes of lightning and claps of thunder
Not even a letter was allowed to pass
No crueler fate could ever surpass
The years dragged by slowly one by one
She grew to be gorgeous and always fun
They each married others as time went by
Raised families but in secret often would cry
Life went on and sure didn't seem fair
The feeling of true love just wasn't there
She never gave up her secret life it seems
Continually searching for the man of her dreams
Sixty years is a mighty long time by rights
It translates into twenty two thousand days and nights
But the roots stayed alive, that flower has bloomed
The spell has withered and died it can be assumed
This couple now talks on a regular basis
Amidst the tedium of living, they are a thriving oasis
Their previous commitments are still in control
But compared to the past they are now on a roll
The chance for their future really looks bright
Though older and slower, they still can excite
In spite of the long long trail back to the past
If it's meant to be, true love will last

Memories Gift

Memories give us pleasures and heart aches
Why do we go back and relive
Why do we re-examine past mistakes
When it's long past time to forgive

There is a well known trail back as far as we can see
It is our personal path to sorrow and satisfaction
A secret place where we are wont to flee
Seeking one last drop of pleasure from an old attraction

That winding trail back to the dark dim past
We cannot close the gate nor should we
We are molded today by all that we have passed
Thus we are different and may not agree

When we take time to pause and reflect
What we remember should only be a guide
The good and the bad as we recollect
Should merge together like a groom and his bride

Afflatus

Darling, you are my inspiration
Pumping the juices of creation
No matter if I feel frustration
Or if I'm soaring with elation
Sometimes I'm sure it's a combination
I remain focused on our destination
As I extol thee in admiration
I contemplate the vagaries of temptation
And relish the sweet aroma of our relation
The world must know of our limitation
But undaunted we continue our preparation
I would send you verses of infatuation
Expressing my love without hesitation
If you find ours to be a weird situation
If you really wonder about our association
Remember it's not good to live in isolation
So consider this as my invitation
No need to worry about the transformation
It'll come naturally with our integration

The Cuddlers

I love to cuddle with you each morning
I love to cuddle with you each night
But the very best cuddling, if I have a choice
Is when you first wake up in the morning
With sleep still in your voice

Remember yesterday when you awoke
While I gently kissed your face
Then I kissed you all over down to your secret place
When you began stretching like a kitten on a rug
We just had to give each other a total body hug

You're so soft and cuddly and smell so damn good
I get intoxicated with your beauty and just being close
So when I act goofy, I hope it's understood
I can never get used to you; I'll never get enough
I especially like you sleeping in the rough

The reason we like to cuddle, it's all part of love
I love my head upon your pillow, my face right next to yours
To look deep into your eyes and see reflected there
The love we have for each other, nothing can compare
To hold you ever closer and know that you are mine

Love is not the author of heartaches or of pain
It will keep us warm and happy like a multicolored quilt
When it's really true love, There's no reason to have guilt
So come rest your weight upon me
We may not know the reason but we know it's meant to be

The Long Road

When Rita and Vic were just sixteen
The long road to the future could not be seen
Their love was so strong, innocent and pure
Life was wonderful, rosy and sure

Now in their sunset, they shouldn't look at the list
Of all that they wanted and all that they missed
Life is still wonderful, rosy but obscure
They only know that their love will endure

All that they missed is just too sad you see
Thinking of now... alas they are not free
Rita and Vic have nothing planned
So they live their lives in fantasyland

Now with graying hair and faltering step
They still view life with lots of pep
They may never consummate what they feel
For the vagaries of life are all too real.

To Dream

Just standing together shoulder to shoulder
Looking together out over the land
Being in her aura, I must hold her
Or feel the touch of her dear hand

I sense the privilege of having her there
Standing with me as though we are one
Glancing down at her graying hair
She's the greatest gift that can't be out done

She asks for little, her wants are small
To life's endeavors one hundred percent
When giving to others, she gives her all
And knows not malice or discontent

I may not have in life's short span
Her with me without reserve
I may just be an also ran
And shouldn't expect what I don't deserve

The moments I've had are my treasure chest
Like jewels and riches beyond compare
Memories give meaning to life's best
To dream, to dream ah—do I dare

A Man And His Horse

There is a journey we all must take
To the land of the great unknown
And this final trip that we must make
We each must make alone

I hope they give me a good horse to ride
Tho I'm in no hurry to take my turn
When its time to cross that great divide
To the land of no return

As I go to meet the great big boss
To tally up my score
Please let me ride my top hoss
And I won't ask for more

All cowboys know when the going is tough
A sure-footed horse knows what to do
The trail may be crooked and rough
No reports have ever come through

Or it could be all flowers and sunshine
With a path by a fresh mountain stream
Still, having a good horse would surely be fine
For a man and his horse are a team

The Sands Of Time

Destiny is never outwitted
No one can alter its plan
The events of life are committed
Puzzle it out if you can
Many obstacles keep us from straying
From destiny's grand design
"what will be will be"is a saying
A saying that keeps us in line
But I know two who've defeated
Destinys course in a way
Against all odds they've cheated
Fate from having her say
All the tricks that fate has mustered
And some mighty twisted I'm sure
Destiny must be all flustered
Wondering how these two endure
Time has taken a beating
They've outlasted the plan you see
They've taken control of their meeting
And destiny has set them free
Love has proven to be stronger
Than chains or iron bands
Even if it must wait longer
til the timer loses its sands

Two Souls Have Touched

Through the swirling sands of time
Out of the murky mists of a distant past
I clearly heard her call my name
"virg" she said she spoke my name at last

And tho memories fade and are soon gone,
When two souls have touched, their love is sound
Their paths have led them far apart
A spring when stretched will rebound

But who is this lovely child of god?
Do I really know her? What is the truth?
I imagine her like the girl I knew
To me there's magic about this girl named Ruth

Hark! a warning bell keeps sounding
Virg, be careful, you can do much wrong
Don't let your selfishness carry the day
Be a gentleman, first and last, be strong

God, if I only knew what course to take
My heart and brain are so diverse
Such strong emotions, long thought dead
I'm as muddled as this rambling verse

Footprints

Two sets of footprints side by side
Tell a story it" s hard to hide
He and she walked together toward tomorrow
Footprints cannot foretell future sorrow

Seeing those prints so close; male and female
From the far distant past tell a poignant tale
Looking back from the future trying to surmise
We can see a couple with hope in their eyes

Now we fast-forward till they're old and grey
Pitifully they're still hoping to have their day
Just reconnected after sixty odd years
"Will life be too short", is one of their fears

As I look at those prints now hardened in stone
I have a great sadness for I am alone
I know the value of a partner; lover and friend
Hope is the elixir that carries us on to the end

The Hand We Were Delt

We shouldn't question the hand we were dealt
Don't bother wondering why some one got more
God knows we can play the cards that we have
Adversity and struggle builds character for sure
And character builds hope in those who endure

If we think opportunity has passed us by
If we know others who have all the luck
The answer of why, we may not be given to know
We can be sure when everything has gone bad
That we are wiser and stronger for the troubles we've had

If we think happiness is getting what we want
When we say, "If only things had been different"
Then we forget that we are part of Gods plan
Let us do the best that we can and not make a fuss
The simplest things in life can bring happiness to us

Prayers For Each Tomorrow

"Fifty years to life", the preacher said
The sentence was heavy upon me the day that she was wed
One day at a time, the years have passed
Hope always lingered from the first day to the last

She's still doing time, fifty years to life
For more than fifty years as someone else's wife
Each day always has a new tomorrow
So far my hopes have all turned to sorrow

How can I plan for tomorrow without you
There is no future that I can ever do
If you're not here with me it seems
At least you're in the forefront of all my dreams

Ice Cold Fingers

Out of the darkness I sensed a coming
With light so dim I could faintly see
Up and down my back a prickling, numbing
An awareness that all was not as it should be

It was a waking dream,I soon realized
I breathed so shallow, short of breath
Unable to move, I sat frozen, paralyzed
With mind racing, was this a messenger of death

Then ice cold fingers gripped me from behind
And a soft voice said 'It's your time you know"
Remembering the unlimited power of Mind
I gasped with conviction, No I cannot go"

"I have an appointment on some future date"
I felt my body starting to float above the chair
"I promised my love that I'd be there, if she could wait
It felt so weird as I seemed to rise and float on air

I pressed my point stating, "God is love
And true love is the strongest of all known power"
Slowly I settled back down from above
My reprieve was complete within the hour

Three Wishes Granted

Ever so softly you spoke to me
With covers pulled up over your head
It started my day with ecstasy
With intimate whispers from your bed

Only a dreamer like me could feel
The closeness your dear voice inspires
You're in my prayers each time I kneel
And the grand prize of my life's desires

Now that I have your love today
I've completely forgotten my other two wishes
I've tossed the old magic lamp away
Back into the sea with the fishes

Old Buck Had To Listen

Tear drops were falling on my saddle
As I rode slowly up the trail
Old Buck with me astraddle
Once more I had no mail

It was over and I had to know it
She was not my girl anymore
I tried so hard not to show it
But I was wounded to the core

It sure hurt when I came to believe
She had another man where I did fail
Several years I had to grieve
While old Buck listened to my tale

Confused

A wise man once sat pondering
How near the future could actually be
Is it always moving, he keeps wondering
Or is it static and the movement just we

We know the poles on the side of the road
Are not really moving as we pass by
So the future may be just a code
Of coming events, there's an endless supply

This wise man is considering a secret plan
To solve the puzzle of what comes next
There has been an order since time began
That cause always comes before effects

What a triumph if that order could be changed
A change of future events before they arrive
All sorts of things could then be arranged
And we would owe this man a big high five

The Thrill Of Discovery

A voyage of discovery just may not be
Seeking new lands over yon horizon
It could be exploring a new friend to see
If we want to strike sails from the mizzen

Or even drop anchor for awhile
Every captain always needs a first mate
Before charting a course to a tropical isle
The thrill of exploring can be better than great

If your ship has been tossing on a rough sea
No voyage is over until you sight land
So proceed with caution, I think you'll agree
'Till you have a first mate that wears your gold band

Tempted

Today I resisted temptation
Today the devil almost had me
He teased me with an alluring expectation
He had me thinking I'd be so happy

Tomorrow I may not be as strong
I almost just kept on driving
Even though I knew it would be wrong
Luckily some reason is still surviving

Else I'd be on the road to Sandy
Never looking back as I roared away
As happy as a kid with candy
Knowing I'd see her by the end of today

Is It Early Or Late?

They say it's darkest before the dawn
Now lets rise and sing our song
Lets retrieve the pieces and carry on
It has been a long night; sixty years long

It was like being put on indefinite hold
Then forgotten as life whizzed by
When nothing happened except growing old
But now we see breaking day in the eastern sky

We are so anxious to start a new day
We are actually prancing at the starting gate
We want it now without further delay
Because we know it will be so great

Certain Thoughts

Certain thoughts can make one squeeze
Not necessarily done just to please
But rather it is an immediate reaction
Perhaps as a prelude to further action

So if you have been so afflicted
Of having those thoughts, you stand convicted
It may remain hidden if you do not tell
Unless someone knows you very very well

You are lucky if you have such a twinge
Just be careful so as not to binge
If you have someone with whom to share
Then you know it's always better as a pair

The Second Time

To have that passion the second time
Is a lot harder than the first
Unless, of course, you have the feeling sublime
That destiny has been reversed

A second chance at first love does
Miracles to strengthen the bond
Memories become so precious because
It's not just the moment but way beyond

Love can be so strong and all consuming
Like a beautiful garden in our care
Where spring flowers are always blooming
And hope eternal is in the air

A Bundle Of Joy

120 lbs in one bundle of joy
Lots of cheer and enthusiasm to enjoy
Ready to greet me with a big wet kiss
There is no love ever better than this

There is such closeness as we bond
Not just for the moment but way beyond
With trust and loyalty unsurpassed
Our collection of memories is so vast

Ah to hold, caress and squeeze
No objections any time I please
Mine to cherish no matter where
Thank you, God, for answering prayer

Summer Love

Oh how I love my summer love
With me through autumn, winter and spring
I rate her love very high above
The necessities of life or anything

Loving me should be her only role
More precious even than food or drink
Her love sustains and nourishes my soul
Without it, I could not survive, I think

New Links In An Old Chain

Overwhelmed with a warm fuzzy feeling
That rises up inside me when I think
About the time I kissed you while kneeling
Each and every thought of you is a connecting link

And each day I always make a very long chain
That would reach from here all the way to Mars
A chain of links where old memories have lain
Covered by the dust of ages and many scars

Yet now new life, new hope is in the air
And an old love is budding with new growth
I know that overwhelming feeling that we share
Builds new memories daily for us both

We've disturbed the dust in a very old tomb
That creaking old door now stands ajar
Peering inside that murky room
Tis not death but life; look a guiding star!

Rainbow Of Colors

My emotions are a multitude of colors
Iridescent like the plumage of a starling
Flickering up and down the scale
Each time I hear you call me darling

Ranging from white of worship and adoration
Thru orange, pink and yellow, degrees of love and possession
Down to the total blackness of desolation
A kaleidoscope of colors from each session

Blue and green may mean logic and reason
Often obscured by the hot red of passion
Call me darling often in any season
The rainbow seems to be my fashion

The Devil Has His Way

The devil sat upon a big black horse
Like Satan himself with just red holes for eyes
As a line of souls trailed slowly by
He counted those he had already bought
And checked off some still worth a try
Dark storm clouds gathered in the west
The sun had already set for those now passing by
From the darkening shadows a banshee wailed
At the fork the right went toward a light
The lost souls were turned to the left into the dark
They were the ones who had failed
Now you know about the left and the right
Once you arrive it's too late to choose
So make your choice early in life

Up Is Better

Why the class distinction between up and down
Up,up,up is always thought the best
Down,down,down downward is not good
The most desirable always seems to be on top
To get a better job is called moving up
The same when getting a bigger house or car
To the soldier up in rank means money and prestige
The students grades place him toward the bottom or the top
We say the homeless person is down and out
And the young exec is climbing the ladder to success
Ever since our ancestors crawled up from the sea
Crawled up to seek the action; up to higher ground
Man has thought that up is good and down definitely is not
We always say up in heaven and down in hell
Down has a stigma; no one wants to go down
With possibly one exception
Going up is better than going down

In Love With My Best Friend

Yes I'm in love with my best friend
If our passion should ebb and flow
She'll be my friend and partner to the end
By my side, together and onward we shall go

They say people change over time
I'll testify many things stay the same
Friendship must be constant else its not worth a dime
In spite of all the love a couple may proclaim

True friendship involves real caring
Treating others opinions with respect
Enjoying another's company and sharing
Loving thoughts may then connect

The Harder The Sweeter

If it seems impossible to some
It's just a bigger challenge with obstacles to overcome
Let your heart and spirit urge you on
Forget "impossible" there's a goal to be won

Yes, nothing is impossible to a willing heart
So don't be timid and afraid to even start
Some things "impossible" come true each day
Perhaps you know of some when you've had your way

So let your heart and spirit be your guide
If you really want it, expand your thinking, open wide
Knowing that you can do it, that's the key
And if its very hard, the sweeter it will be

The Octogenarians

Two octogenarians stood at last
In a little white church before the alter
They had waited while many generations passed
And had walked down the isle without a falter

They clung to each other as they said their vows
She carried a small bouquet on her arm
No family or friends with raised eyebrows
Her gaze was steady with her hand on his forearm

At the end they turned and kissed as your supposed to do
Arm in arm they started back toward the open door
The preacher had blest and marveled at these two
Suddenly she gasped and sank slowly to the floor

He knelt to lift her but she would not waken
Instinctively he knew that she had passed
He sobbed and cried aloud to also be taken
He knew her tired old heart had beat its last

Peering through the window was an ugly ole dragon
Though he had won, he shed a few tears
As he went down the road with his tail a draggen
He had grown fond of this couple after so many years

Heaven

There's a place called heaven and I've been there
It's not far off like a foreign land
But very close and near at hand
I was taken by a little girl with silver hair
With her head upon my pillow
She gazed into my eyes and said
"Hi, I love being in your bed
Few men have ever known how sweet an angel can be
Or have ever felt the magic touch of their hand
A touch that can make ones flesh expand
Or know their hot breath upon your face is ecstasy
Heaven I think may be only a feeling
From knowing you're loved by beauty and perfection
Knowing you have everything upon reflection
Will float your spirit up near the ceiling
I so love the beauty of her darling face
And appreciate the nuances of her female form
Snuggled next to me cuddly and warm
Only separated from heaven by a small piece of lace

We Are Immortal

The cell appears immortal so why do we age
Because we are convinced and really believe
That death is the inevitable last stage
Our mortal mind seems programmed to deceive

We are made of the spirit and likeness of GOD
We don't have to get sick or wither away
Remember the story of Erin's rod
Which budded, blossomed and brought forth fruit in a day

All things are perfect which GOD has made
If only we not let mortal perception interfere
Not easy, of course, when so much is displayed
To imperfect mind causes imperfection to appear

The Way I Am

You are the way you are and I'm glad
You're not with me every moment of every hour, I'm sad
We talk and make plans, I'm beaming
To make things happen, I end up scheming

When things are going our way, I'm pleased
Your always willing; I never have to say I've been teased
When we know we are going to meet, I'm cheerful
But when you have to go away, I'm tearful

When you tell me what you want, I'm willing
When our thoughts turn into action, I find it thrilling
When you whisper in my ear, I get horny
What ever else they may say about me, I'm corny

Day Dreams

Dark shadows have long obscured
Old dreams that somehow endured
When out of the darkness pale and wan
Barely alive, they arose to stretch and yawn

Old dreams that we are nurturing again
Even more precious now than they were back then
Like a spring plant sprouting new buds
The dam has broken; they're coming in floods

Old dreams and new are a potent mix
Especially now that we know some new tricks
We'll not be deterred, we're here to stay
Our dreams will become reality someday

Ruth

One of the great curiosities of the day
That taxes my mental capacity
Why she sees herself in such a way
While gifted with a bulldogs tenacity

She doesn't know she's as cute as a speckled pup
But sees herself as old and gray
Others opinions are on the up and up
Everyone sees her as pretty and gay

Tho I'm not just a casual observer
I'm well aware of her classical beauty
As she lives her life with zest and fervor
Never forgetting her sense of duty

I always think of her as pretty, pretty, pretty
She can't believe it and that's a pity
She's so darn cute, charming and witty
And much better cuddling than any kitty

Afterward

WOW! We have just finished
My energy level is so diminished
It's very hard to stay awake
But I can't miss the icing on the cake

With half-closed eyes I am peeping
At you dear while you're sleeping
I love your sweet smile of satisfaction
You stroke my ego with this reaction

The choicest words I ever expect to hear
Were simply when you said "Thank you dear"
No man has ever been more blest
Than I with your head upon my chest

The Prettiest Flower

Of all beautiful flowers that have come my way
There is one stands out above all the rest
Always the brightest in any bouquet
A symbol of Gods handiwork at its best

Gently caressed by life's every breeze
Tormented by the gusty winds of love
This delicate flower has been able to please
And continued to thrive as a gentle dove

This wild flower attracts me like a honey bee
Wanting to taste the sweetest honey
I'm buzzing around where all can see
My little flower loves it warm and sunny

Holy Cow!!

Today I see a sky with the brightest blue
A lilac with the deepest purple
And all the flowers have the prettiest hue
A bird is singing the loveliest song
All the people have such a friendly smile
This is the world where I belong
The mountains and the valleys look so grand
I see the real beauty in this desert
I have an affinity with this land
Quietly I hear the cooing of a dove
I can't stop my feet from dancing
I know it's because I am in love

Unknown Mysteries

Undiscovered ideas have a special appeal
Can an ordinary thinker like me conjure
Up amazing new ideas with which we deal
Or develop a unique twist to a theory de jour

In the pond of pre-discovery I love to fish
In its murky depths is a mysterious contender
Of all weird things I can imagine, I surely wish
I could understand "branes" a true mind-bender

The Hamburger Tree

Few are they who ever knew
About the hamburger tree and where it grew
It's a secret my dear that you and I share
We know exactly what it is and where

I've seen some strange things as a human bean
This is one of the strangest I've ever seen
You created it with such loving care
It's my treasure, the rarest of the rare

Unlike other trees, it seems to shrink
Almost daily it's getting smaller I think
The tribulations of life go on and on
I fear one day it'll be completely gone

The Stars Know

I had no compass to guide me
No stars to point the way
Just a lonely wanderer
With no plans to mark each day

Then a senorita said she loved me
A senorita from days of yore
She set my heart to beating
Like it had never beat before

Now I'm far from aimless
Now I certainly have a goal
She has given me good reason
To really search my soul

Surprised at what I found there
The real love I've always had
Suppressed, I thought it hopeless
Now there's hope and I'm so glad

Now when I look at the heavens
And thank the good Lord above
The stars are winking at me
Because they know that I'm in love

Communing With Nature

Thunder rumbled loudly in the night
Dark storm clouds obscured the sky
Flashes of lightening split the darkness
Somewhere a child began to cry

As though something strange was impending
I stood watching and delighting
As the forces of nature were at play
At once eerily foreboding, yet exciting

It must be the pagan within me
I wanted to dance naked in the rains
To dance wildly in abandon
With hot blood pumping through my veins

The Squeeze

With her tiny hand in mine
I'm thrilled to feel her loving squeeze
A tingling up and down my spine
How eagerly she wants to please

Sweet music is her lilting laughter
Oh, how I love to feel her squeeze
I remember its message for long after
As I see her hair trembling in the breeze

She is the prettiest thing I've ever seen
I'll never forget how it feels to have her squeeze
For sure she is my loving queen
Perhaps I should address her on my knees

With her strong arms about me
I know I'm going to feel her squeeze
Strongly loving each other is the key
For together we are always so at ease

Many are they who see her beauty and grace
But only I am thrilled to feel her squeeze
As she pulls me into her warm embrace
My temperature rises by several degrees

A Secret Place

I rode the wave of exhilaration
When she said, "I love you dear"
Soaring high with my elation
I wanted all the world to hear

Alas! For now our love is forbidden
There is a secret place we know
A chamber that is quite well hidden
Our secret plans are there to go

A place where no one can find us
We'll have our memories to remind us
Then put our past lives behind us
No cares if hot passion will blind us

Is It A Sure Bet?

She wears the band of bondage on her finger
It should be a warning to those who want to linger
But there's a wild young cowboy who dares to stay
No one can persuade him to just go away

He'll risk it all for a fleeting taste of honey
More important than life or fame or money
Determined to win the prize, he'll take a chance
For this beautiful doll, he is willing to bet the ranch

What Happened

What has happened to my valley
Why is the sunshine no longer warm
I used to linger and dilly dally
And watch the birds and squirrels perform

Now I no longer see all of the beauty
The grass, trees and mountains are just there
The colors in the sunset are no longer pretty
Now a strange haze seems to dull the air

It all changed as soon as Ruth was gone
I miss her sweet smile and gentle touch
No enthusiasm now but I must carry on
Ruth brought to this valley love, zest and beauty and such

A Toast

I raise my glass to toast the girl
That has set my mind atwitter
I'm not sure if I come or go
But I know she is no quitter

She set her sights a long time ago
On something that she really wanted
When it was snatched right from her grasp
She persevered undaunted

She now has me wrapped around her finger
I'm all hers anytime she wants to beckon
Just when, I suppose nobody knows
But she'll have me someday I reckon

The Joy Of Life

I've reached the stage where I can smile
As I look fate in the eye the while
Tho she has won the first round or two
I have finally prevailed because of you

Others will age and then they'll die
But we've overcome that mortal lie
The love we share has turned us around
As we grow younger, the signs abound

God's love has given us our time at last
God knows we've endured a very long fast
There is joy now in each breath I take
The richness of life is ours to partake

The Silent Cry

The sanctuary of home is the greatest treasure
Where we can retreat from the world outside
Comfort and solace of loved ones in some measure
Familiarity and security where we abide

But pity those who have no home
No ties to family or their own place
Often by choice each day they roam
With no one to touch, never an embrace

They are truly lost in this old world
Their souls must ache and they know not why
Their minds are numbed and figuratively curled
In a fetal position as they silently cry

A Vacant Stare

I once saw a man who wasn't there
His somber eyes moved so slow
Not sharp quick eyes darting everywhere
There are some wounds that do not show

His shoulders drooped as in defeat
I wondered what had happened, what circumstance
Was there a crisis he could not meet
Had there been so much that he saw no chance

I think he had lost all sense of hope
What he had lost he could not regain
His will was gone, he could not cope
A hidden wound with searing pain

Help Available

Darling, I send these stories with all due respect
If some you can't "get", as I suspect
Rather than have you fret and tax your brain
Just give me a call and I'll explain

Many things in this world are very complex
That's why men are here to help the weaker sex
I'm always here when you have a need
Your plea for help I'll quickly heed

Life On The Edge

I tremble when I consider my dear
That I could exit this life without you near
In spite of all I can possibly do
Could it be that I'll never have you

Nay, say it isn't so; it cannot be
Of all sad fates chosen for you and me
There must be a future to contemplate
A future when you will actually be my mate

When I think of all this in a positive way
My trembling stops for awhile, for a day
If ever we stop living our lives on the edge
My total love is all yours, I pledge

What If

If I could listen to your private thoughts,
Would you let me?
If I could tune in as you soak in the tub,
Would you let me?
If I could read your thoughts as you lie in bed,
Would you let me?
If I could know what you're thinking anytime I choose,
Would you let me?

I only ask such things, my dear, because
I know you would
If I ask you to give me a passionate kiss,
I know you would
If I ask you for a total body hug,
I know you would
If I ask that you forever love me,
I know you would

If you think I'm taking you too much for granted,
Perhaps I am
If you think I'm really too conceited,
Perhaps I am
If you think I'm just a silly romantic,
Perhaps I am
If you think I'm head over heels in love,
Of course I am

A Lonesome Wail

She and I once played with fire
And lost all control of our desire
Taking no heed as flames licked higher
Dancing in the glow of cautions pyre

Now with emotions left hanging high
Where is the sun in our cloudy sky
It matters not that we know why
We are denied that for which we cry

If you hear a lonesome wail
Please shed a tear for this sad tale
Of lovers who lost because of mail
Now live in limbo much like jail

The Bidet

My lady was out one day
And since I'm a curious sort
I decided to try her bidet
If you're interested, this is my report

The water was cold and such a shock
I got all wet; it wasn't any fun
I jumped and grabbed my sock
Embarrassed by what I had done

In mopping up I slipped and fell
Hobbled with my pants down to the floor
I gave myself a big black eye, oh well
I'll not try that again, no never more

Eager Kisses

Eager kisses I know are waiting
They are the icing when we are dating
The loveliest lips I've ever seen
They first touched mine when she was fifteen

Gently caressing lips with lips
With her standing on tippy toe tips
Then hungrily we each devour
The taste of love; 'tis our hour

While her twinkling eyes look into mine
Her hot breath more heady than wine
Ah! Those eager kisses from my colleen
I love that girl, she is my queen

Treasures

As our treasures of love mount ever higher
Our blessings accrue from many places
Giving us most of what we desire
And many of our heartaches it erases

Among the treasures we can count
Is a closeness we can never describe
It has brought us to the elixir of life's fount
With the promise of eternal youth as we imbibe

One of our great blessings we have learned
We receive help from the spiritual side
Many things happen where our love is concerned
Almost as if we've been given a guide

Remembering When

I think of you each time I shave
And stand there by the sink
I'll remember it till I'm in the grave
It usually turns my face to pink

As I think of the things we've done
As we strove to get acquainted
I assure you you're the only one
With another I would have fainted

So come my dear and let us try
Something sexy that we can do
Unless of course you are too shy
About intimacy between us two

The Sultan

The Sultan of wonderland says
The reason he's Sultan and not the pres
Is that no one votes in wonderland
People just come and go unplanned

The Sultan has been there much longer
And his wonderings keep getting stronger
Than those in dreamland next door
Who can dream and reality ignore

The Sultan keeps wondering just when
And wondering about what might have been
That's why the Sultan is in charge
Tho his harem is certainly not large

One beauty is all he can handle
As no other can hold a candle
Because her charms are so alluring
So enticing and forever enduring

Captain

Am I the captain of my ship
Is it I who decides to take the trip
Or are decisions made by a higher source
Just how and when to chart my course

It's hard to know which choice is right
I can't always be the shinning knight
But once in awhile would be nice
To know instead of rolling the dice

There is a huge decision I must make
It's so important, so much at stake
I'm only kidding myself, I guess
This isn't like a game of chess

Why try to analyze my every move
When it is my heart that must approve
Therefore, dear heart, the choice is made
Reason lost; love has by far outweighed

The Next Page

The next page I can't wait to see
As night turns to day, it gives to me
An exciting chance to learn whatever will be
The mystery of what's next is the key

The key to my joy is that I'm expecting
Wonderful times await me, I'm projecting
All the signs are there that I'm detecting
Happy moments like dots I'll be connecting

My life's story is an open book to read
Some pages tell of what I need
Others recount what has made me bleed
But the future is where it's at, I'll concede

Tsunami

I was bowled over by a giant wave
That left me gasping for air
I didn't even see it coming
I was caught completely unaware

I'm a simple man with simple tastes
But beauty and sex hit me all at once
I know not what came over me
Thus I continue to babble like a dunce

That tsunami has borne me to an incredible high
Sustained I'm sure by our frequent calls
And my remembrance of her legendary beauty
And her picture that hangs in these hallowed halls

Ghost Dancers

The ghost dancers are out tonight
In the flickering shadows of my camp fire
How eerily they prance in the darkness of night
As I add more wood, they leap ever higher

With my back to the chill north wind
I stare into the fire hypnotic
Daydreaming of a girl, I pretend
And those ghost dancers dance so chaotic

The ghost dancers are cheery in away
They keep me from being alone
At first light they begin to fade into day
The sun always dispels the unknown

Blurred Vision

I see her coming toward me
But my vision is very unclear
All objects seem to be blurring
Why is it I can hardly see

I rub my eyes and find they are not dry
I guess I'm such a sissy because
I'm so darn glad to see her but
Why should joy make me cry?

Wisdom Of The Ages

Sensually her look and touch
Tell me she reads my thoughts and such
She has the collective wisdom of all
Women down through the ages on which to call

She seems to sense without being told
That we are kindred spirits both new and old
Of her innate knowledge, I stand in awe
On the instinct of a million generations, she can draw

I thank the Lord I am her man
Trying to understand as best I can
The message here that I want to convey
Is simply, "I love her in my humble way"

Hyperclose

No lifetime memories for us to share
We can only imagine all the things we didn't do
Our recent memories are beyond compare
Everything we do is to us so new

I coined a new term to describe our relation
Hyperclose defines where we're at today
Very very close, yet far across the nation
How close most words can't begin to say

As close as to peas in a pod, the saying goes
We're also as much alike as those two peas
Our private thoughts the other always knows
What one wants the other knows how to please

Innocence

There is nothing like the innocence of a little girl
And when she trustingly placed her hand in mine
My heart melted as I looked down on this little one
I felt an urge to protect her from life's cruel design

She shouldn't have to worry about turmoils in life
I hoped her path would always be milk and honey
I hoped I could always be there to smooth her way
And supply all her needs, be it love or money

She has experienced this world for awhile
She may know what certain feelings are all about
Tho she's a great grandmother several times over
She still needs all of my love without any doubt

Cowboys And God

High up in the Rubies, a cowboy rested his horse
Beside an ice-cold stream just below where it begun
Just below the snow bank which is the waters source
Far below the valley simmered in the desert sun

If you have ever been there, then you know who's in control
That is why cowboys can really appreciate God
Especially why cowboys have poetry in their soul
For God has marked the trail that most cowboys have trod

Cowboys are often sweaty and covered with dust and dirt
Some times they cuss and maybe broke as hell
Some of them are ugly; some have manure on their shirt
But God seems to love them no matter how they smell

If you know a cowboy, try to look inside
Outside he may appear to be rough and tough
Pay no attention to scars and scratches on his hide
Somewhere you'll find he's a gentleman sure enough

Our Syrup

Like sweet syrup thick and protective
I could feel it about me loving and warm
It had substance; was real from my perspective
It appeared with your phone call in early morn

No one can see it but it is so real
An absolute closeness between you and me
It's your love that I reach out and feel
Not just a little but the nth degree

I know without saying that you sense it too
That my love surrounds you wherever you are
I want to be as close as any tattoo
Across the miles I'll hug you, however bizarre

The Reason Why

She repeatedly asks how we have arrived
At the impasse we are in today
Now that our connection has been revived
So close and yet there is no way

But if our course is set by Gods great plan
If we are here to grow and learn
Consider our opportunity now if you can
There are certain truths we can discern

Daily our connection grows stronger
We're forced to contemplate the spiritual and mystical
And for sure, each day our connection is longer
And we are less distracted by the physical

Now I can appreciate that inner jewel
Hidden within your secret vault
I find the essence of you so cool
It's the spiritual you that I exalt

If the time ever comes that we kiss and touch
Our souls have married in the spiritual sense
I miss you darling, so very very much
And think of us now in the future tense

Adventure Is Our Prey

We are animals, my dear, in a way
We have a hunger unsatisfied
Together we are stalking our prey
We'll do what it takes, we're not dignified

We' re stalking an adventure so wild
When we find it, then we will pounce
We want nothing too timid or mild
The thrill of the chase is what counts

We don't ask permission to go out to play
Our games are no longer that of a kitten
Stealthily we've escaped to a secret hideaway
And are reviewing the list we have written

How exciting to finally get started at last
Exploring together what lies before us
It's like disrobing, we've now shed our past
Our faith and time will completely restore us

So take my paw my little feline
Get ready to pounce on our quarry
Together our prowess always shine
Let the unbelievers be wary

You Give Me Pride

You may not be perfect but then
You're certainly close enough for me
Your sweetness exceeds all I ken
 I would not change any part of thee

Of great importance to any man is pride
You bolster mine just being by my side
It honors me when you hold my hand
I feel important and in command

All I have to offer thee is love
Which you shall always have my little dove
Onward and upward we shall go
Buoyed by how freely our love does flow

Angels

Angels smile when flowers bloom
And they smile when she enters the room
Angels love the breath of spring
And all the beauty that joy will bring

My girl brings beauty just being there
She gives it to others with her touch and care
Her goodness gives the angels pause
They gather around her just because

She's an example of Gods perfect hand
Such a beautiful life in a troubled land
I for one will surely attest
That of all the angels, she is the best

What Is Too Old?

If you would shed a tear for two
Who are pathetic in their dream
They keep planning but have no clue
That they are chasing a hopeless scheme

So much time has already gone
They are not concerned how much is left
They encourage each other and carry on
But chances are they'll be bereft

Hope is eternal they always say
But it is sad when there is little chance
God bless them now they are old and gray
Surely too old for any romance

Passion

It's so great to feel excitement and passion
To feel blood surging through my veins
For timid souls I have compassion
But give me a way to loose my chains

Let me tap my inner power
And energize that driving force
I look forward to my finest hour
With trust in God as my resource

Steering safely through every storm
I relish the fervency of desire
Such thoughts keep my passion warm
As I think of her who fuels this fire

Who Am I?

By the flames of fire have I been tried
And tempered by the course of life
I've been hammered and chiseled when I was down
I've had and lost and tried again
I should be hard and cynical for where I've been
But I'm a softie, I can't explain
I cry at another's tale of woe
I cry at movies and anything sad
My emotions are always ready to flow
I can't play poker; I'm an open book
Just look in my eyes if you wonder who I am
You can see I want to be your friend

The Importance Of Design

The council met to try to decide
The weighty question of who designed
What we collectively know as woman kind
Experts were called to express their view
So the council could benefit from what each knew
First was an artist who discussed every part
Pointing out her curves and beauty were a work of art
He was sure the artist had shown his hand
To make her form so appealing to every man
The curves and symmetry of each lovely part
Was the purest art right from the heart
The next to speak was an engineer
With charts and drawings he made it clear
The reason all of her parts worked so fine
Was the engineering skill used in her design
How the ball and socket joints rotated about
He spoke of leverage and fulcrums that made her stout
And the counter weight in the rear, he began to tell
Was to keep her balanced when her belly begins to swell
Finally to make their research complete was their plan
So they sought the ideas of a common man
They were totally surprised to hear his decision
That she was designed by the regional planning commission
When queried, his answer gave them all hysteria
Because, he said, who else would place a disposal
System right next to a recreational area?

What We Never Had

The seasons come and the seasons go
I still miss all the things we never had
No decades of memories for me to know
Only lost opportunities that make me sad

A million things that add up to life
Can never be shared by you and me
The successes, the heartaches, the joy and strife
Were not there for us and never will be

Let us toast to the dreams we never knew
Then let us forget what we never had
To such useless thoughts, we'll bid adieu
Of our fresh start we arc certainly glad

There is much to be said for a new beginning
Making plans and testing the water
The game never ends during the first inning
So let's go for it doing what we aughter

Are We There Yet?

Are we there yet ?
Anxious words oft repeated
Children are prone to fret
When will their journey be completed

Grown ups too find it hard to wait
To savor the reality of their dreams
Always prancing at the starting gate
Time can be an eternity it seems

It's good to still be a kid at heart
To experience the joy of anticipation
Ah! the enthusiasm it does impart
Knowing success will bring elation

The Power Of A Symbol

Trustingly, she placed her hand in mine
As I looked down to see them together
Small and firm, it fit so fine
I felt no doubts as to whether

They belonged thus clasped forever
The message it sent was perfect content
To never be without her, no never
As my love upsurged one hundred percent

Yet, it was a symbol so simple
So trusting and giving so freely
I caressed her fair cheek, her smile and her dimple
And silently thanked God, yes really

The Traveler

I'm a traveler and I've been stranded
The year of 2003 is where I've landed
I had gone back to the forties to make a change
Illegal, of course, and the effect was strange
It caused my time-warp generator to fail
I've tried to restart it to no avail
Time spun to a crawl in a dizzying whirl
Stranding me here " cause of a very pretty girl
She was only sixteen, when I saw her last
Now suddenly sixty years have already passed
Unless I can get a titanium circuit programmed for time
I'll be stuck here paying for my crime
Since it's here I am destined to survive
I'll search for that old lady, if she is still alive
I hope I can find her and hope to see
Some sign that she still remembers me
Is it too much to hope that we can start from here
So I may continue with the girl I hold dear

Sunshine

I call her sunshine
To be near her is my joy
Her pretty smile is her sign
Love bubbling over is pure joy

Bright eyes that say I love you
My heaven could be here and now
If we were together, just us two
If she was only mine somehow

The Massage

There is something quite sexy about a foot massage
 Both for the massageor and the massagee
A massageor can relish the touch of a female foot
Gently caressing her skin, her toes, her heel and her sole
Then firmer and deeper to the muscles inside
While watching her face for the pleasure it evokes
Your touch can be loving and conveys that feeling
So if you find it sexy and sensuous and really do care
She'll know it immediately and enjoy it the more
Another thing a massageor can do, if he be that bold
Is massage those tendons clear up to her calf
With your hands on her calf and her foot on your chest
You're well on the way, whatever your quest

Beauty Is Life

Since longevity is associated with beauty
I expect to be around for quite a spell
My association with her, a real cutie
Is a real advantage, I can already tell

Ahead now lies the rather pleasant task
Of keeping our association beautiful too
The reason it's important, in case you ask
Is so it will last forever as we shall do

Positive is beautiful; that is the key
We used to think we were in the sunset of our day
But darkness has faded, it's dawn you see
There is a lifetime before us, what more can I say

Before The Snow Comes Next Year

They hope to be married before the snow comes next year
Yes, they are planning to wed as you probably will hear
Rita is a lady so sweet and so fine
The sound of her laughter is simply divine

They hope to be married before the snow comes next year
Their love has endured for so long it is clear
Vic is her lover who lives far away
They've waited for this fifty-eight years and a day

They hope to be married before the snow comes next year
If only they can last after getting so near
Vic is an old man with hair that is gray
But they love with a passion that won't go away

They hope to be married before the snow comes next year
If God doesn't favor them, there'll be many a tear
Their love hasn't faded it has only grown stronger
The big question is, do they have to wait longer

A Gleam In Her Eye

Have you noticed, Ruth has a special gleam
A real twinkle in her eye
Some may wonder if she has achieved her dream
Some may just wonder why

Have you noticed she has a spring in every step
She has things to do and places to go
Now more than ever, she's so full of pep
Don't you wonder what gives her this glow

Ruth has a secret she can never tell
What ever it is, it must be a doosy
That makes life so good for this little belle
Not easy to please, she has always been choosy

Ruth knows her own mind; not easy to sway
She's the center of attraction in any crowd
With the wiles of a woman, come what may
Just to know her makes one so proud

Overwhelmed

I have felt so overwhelmed of late
The plasma of life has enveloped me
Warm, all-consuming, I feel the weight
Not an ethereal love; one I can feel and see

The object of my love embodies all good
Thus giving to good form and substance too
The ravages of time and space our love withstood
Because it permeates our existence through and through

Like the warmth of a fire soaking in
My love is not limited to thought or mind
Rather it's everywhere in and out and in again
The sum total of our souls and bodies combined

The Alternate View

As we look back to the love we remember
Untimely severed in one cold December
The view is cloudy and covered with mist
And colored by thoughts of all that we missed

The enormous lapse of time has eroded
Memories have dimmed and been corroded
Now suddenly bright in the "now" of today
We're still aware of the past in a very fond way

But our faces have turned with a forward look
What our future holds could sure fill a book
The big medicine of hope makes us grow younger
As we strive to allay our great hunger

Souls

Of souls I propose the following theory
That we exist here and in a higher dimension too
You may think this all sounds quite eerie
The sense of soul may be the only connection through

A parallel universe with our doubles so very near
Perhaps only a scant centimeter away
Of course we can never see or touch or hear
We sense they're there and call them souls I say

Souls, whatever they may be
Were not intended to live alone
If calling them our alter ego is the key
We're still attached to our flesh and bone

How independent are we from our souls
Maybe a little or a lot or maybe we're not
Perhaps we live life's parallel roles
Somewhat connected but different paths we've sought

When souls touch souls in a special way
Then they're very close I believe
Which affects us here come what may
And neither one ever wants to leave

That First Step

Our love and this moment in time
Are well matched in abstraction
When our ancestors first crawled up out of the slime
It was like this moment a precursor to all the action

The new age was about to begin
What a glorious future and we didn't even know
Ready for adventure as we shed our scales for skin
In today's moment we're poised ready to go

A glorious future awaits for the strong at heart
Our love is ready for its first step upon the land
Ready for all the action; ready to start
Our greatest adventure is very near at hand

Ecstasy

Up close and personal is the feeling
That always sets my senses reeling
When she offers me her lips to kiss
It's truly heaven to experience this

So free and eager is her giving
With a capitol L, I call this Living
She sacrifices so much for me
To bring me bliss and ecstasy

When her beautiful lips touch mine
I feel tingles up and down my spine
Her warm kisses come from the heart
For a moment we¹ re one ere we must part

The End Of The Rainbow

Long have I followed a rainbow
Searching for that pot of gold
For many years I've looked high and low
Knowing that the legend is very old

One day an old leprechaun said, "just follow me"
He led me to a hidden forest glade
I saw the end of a rainbow as plain as could be
And there sat an angel, a beautiful little maid

I knew she was the treasure I'd always heard about
Guarding her, a vicious dragon lay curled up in the shade
He had smoke and fire coming from his snout
I tip toed closer to where his tail laid

When he saw me, he jumped up on all fours
Oh! How I trembled, I really was afraid
Then he broke the silence with his mighty roars
Roars that literally shook this hidden forest glade

I looked at the old leprechaun, he was dancing about with glee
You cant trust a leprechaun, they'll always play a trick
The lovely maiden sadly waved so wistfully
I could go no further; it really made me sick

Then she shouted," We'll just have to wait"
Those were the words that ole dragon wanted to hear
He didn't want that angel to ever have her mate
Thus you know why we named him, it should be clear

Hope

Of all the attributes to which man can attest
Certainly hope is one of the best

It goes with the soldier into battle
And encourages the baby reaching for his rattle

Of course it's hope that urges the gambler on
The same hope of an athlete in a triathlon

Hope is with the bride approaching the alter
And supports the groom so he doesn't falter

It's the hope of man that builds nations
And highlights all aspects of human relations

We should think of hope as our best friend
For without hope, it would be a dismal end

We're all in this world under sentence of death
I ask that hope be with all during their last breath

Heading West

I would ride off into the sunset
With her thigh next to my thigh
Two hearts pounding fast and yet
We are both on a dizzying high

Driving toward that old setting sun
Toward a future we can't comprehend
One moment thinking, "What have we done"
Knowing this is real and no longer pretend

We aren't kids just running away
Though our grandkids might think it so
We've waited and dreamed for many a day
She's my girl and I'm her beau

Wild Flower

There is a wild flower that blooms
Ever so sweetly in sun or shade
When her beauty and fragrance one consumes
Of these things, exotic dreams are made

This wild flower is the rarest of the rare
Ever so elegant in a desert land
Truly no others can compare
I thrill to hold her in my hand

She's my wild flower with visage fair
Forever endowed with the bloom of youth
However clothed or even bare
I love the little wild flower called Ruth

The Shower

Remember...in the shower last night
When our bodies were soapy and wet
Remember the feel of slithering tight
As soapy flesh against flesh met

And the pool of water between your breasts
That we both looked down to see
As the warm water collected between our chests
And the wettest kiss that you gave to me

We caressed and hugged; the water was hot
And the shower was filled with steam
Not only the water was getting hot
As we stood lost in dream

Then I dried your skin til it was pink
And kissed your neck and pert little nose
Then I set you up, upon the sink
And knelt to dry your toes

The Sound Of Her Laughter

I love the sound of her laughter
It's sweet music to my ears
It echoes in my mind long after
And uplifts me when loneliness nears

I hope GOD knows how much I love her
How desperate I become to hear her voice
I hope he knows how much one can need another
And saves her for me if there is a choice

Her chuckles ripple like running water
And freshen my spirit like a mountain stream
Her sparkling eyes like Venus' s daughter
Sooth my breast like a warm sun beam

Her cheerful spirit excites my soul
This young woman reflects GOD's perfection
She keeps the joy of living on a roll
And gives life meaning and direction

Her small and lithesome body is where
My ideal and perfect girl resides
If ever we meet "way out there"
I hope she still loves me, what ere betides

The 11th Hour

There is a look upon your face I adore
That look of love that melts my heart to the core
That look that drives all of the clouds away
And erases all shadows from my day

If God offered me only one wish to make
I'd ask for us a new life span to take
Then we'd escape these boundary walls
And have a full life before God calls

I wouldn't even ask that he change the past
Just give us some time when it's our turn at last
Of all sad things would you believe
In the sunset of life, there's no reprieve

Life's span is short like that of a flower
We've now found each other but in the 11th hour
And even now we are kept apart
Our life is on hold and can't yet start

Some may see in this the irony
To us it's a mixture of joy and agony

We're not happy with the status quo
Still it gives us pleasure, that we know

Cellular Memory

Cellular memory I'm told is a fact
More than our brains tell us how to act
All of our cells, each tiny part
Control our emotions, especially the heart

Each cell remembers its duty in the past
And strives to continue in the role it was cast
That's why Indians ate the buffalo heart
To take on his strength and courage in part

Organ transplants have proved this case
Recipients have changed to match the pace
And feel a kinship to the former owner
And assume characteristics of their donor

All people may be connected in a way
Especially those who have shared DNA
The more they share; the more they're the same
How they think; how they play the game

Dreams

Here's to all the dreams that I have had
That have floated through my mind
Some have lingered since I was a lad
And some I have left far behind

These dreams have shaped my life today
Chasing dreams is what I do
There is always new ones that come my way
Those who know me are affected too

I would not trade my life of dreams
For a dull routine with no hope of change
Sometimes I plan for years it seems
So many goals that I work to arrange

If in my life, you are a part
Then I hope you are a dreamer too
We'll have adventure right from the start
So many opportunities, so much to do

Clasping Hands

Two hands clasping can say so much
In my minds eye I can see
Two hands holding with a loving touch
And the closeness it brings we all agree

Yes, I can see those hands clasping tight
His much larger from years of work
Hers are smaller delicate and light
Also long years of work they did not shirk

Those loving hands now show their age
Somewhat gnarled and bony, yes
Their scars tell life's stories page by page
A gentle squeeze and caring love they express

Palm to palm with fingers interlaced
No longer fresh smooth skin of an earlier year
On those lines their hopes and dreams are traced
What is that drop that fell, is it a tear?

The Yellow Robe

Separate we are, yet so connected
We are so close we're almost one
Same thoughts when reflected
We agree on what is our fun

The great spirit blessed us with a smile
And gave us time to get to know
The joy of closeness so worthwhile
And the thrill a touch can bestow

Wherever we are around the globe
There are tokens we have to remind
Touching my shirt is a yellow robe
And see-through lace left behind

Darling our souls are welded tight
Strengthened and tested for many years
It's our destiny and we know it's right
As we slowly part that veil of tears

And when that veil is fully parted
Dispersing heart aches from long ago
We'll have no reason to be down-hearted
We'll be free to let our love show

A Wrinkle In Space

One day when I was out walking
Late in the day after sun down
I stopped when I heard someone talking
I turned slowly and looked all around

No one near, that was a surprise
Suddenly I felt a chill wind blowing
Eerily the hair on my neck started to rise
I took a step forward not knowing

Why this strange feeling, I could not surmise
The chill wind was fast getting colder
And now something was affecting my eyes
Carefully I sat down upon a large boulder

I heard people talking to each other
AS I listened, my vision started to clear
Then I saw I was somewhere else, oh brother
Carefully I stood and looked to the rear

I knew I must act quickly, but what to do
A wrinkle in space can disappear fast
I took a step backward then two
I returned to the future, much time had passed

Friends said I had been gone for 35 days
For me it was only a minute or so
It's tempting to think there might be ways
To skip a long wait and immediately go

To that future we're all waiting for

The Flames Of Fire

One little spark can surely start
A mighty big fire
Though just sixteen, she set that spark
Igniting my desire

She set it with her flashing smile
And the aura of a woman child
Time has been her friend, the while
Now a woman with the aura of the girl who smiled

I've always loved this comely lass
And will 'til the day I die
She's the epitome of a girl with class
The fire has welded our souls; I'm her guy

A Haunting Look

There is a haunting look behind her eyes
What failed dreams does it conceal
Her beautiful face with lines of laughter
Yet soft and feminine; so utterly dear
Beautiful eyes bright and searching
There is more to her story than they will tell
I long to know her very soul
To understand why each thought is there
Past experiences are hers only
I have no right her past to share
Perhaps I can obscure any lingering sadness
New hope, new dreams are the ultimate cure
Perhaps I'm seeing my own reflection
Is it my haunting, not hers that lingers still?

Lets Waltz

Come my dear and dance with me
Press your body close to mine
Moving as one, our souls are free
Cheek to cheek is so divine

As we sway to a lovers tune
There is ultimate closeness that we feel
Love drops in our path are strewn
The heat we generate we can't conceal

Come my dear and squeeze my hand
That look in your eyes really says it all
We can make music without the band
Each to each our souls enthrall

My Girl

She bade me listen and there would appear
Echoes in my memory from a long dead past
Like a faint drum-beat growing near
Rippling through my mind, first slow then fast

She held my hand as we sat quietly for awhile
Remembering, together lifting that moldering veil
Thoughts occasionally punctuated by a flickering smile
So very far back down that lonesome ole trail

Those haunting echoes will always be there
Reverberating through our minds bitter and sweet
Can we ever reconcile then and now as we share
Old memories while building new is neat

As our new life starts to take hold
With everything different, everything new
Let memories return us often to days of old
Back to the beginning when our love was so new

An Ancient Dream

That ancient dream is off the shelf
We've dusted and polished anew
See that long cemented crack
It happened when it once fell
Rusted and pitted from long ago
Its now starting to shine
By gosh, it shines like new

Mystery In Our History

We are a couple with a history
Not together because of a mystery
Unsolved for fifty eight years
Affecting so many lives, so many tears

Now we strive to pick up the pieces
And learn about kids,grandkids,cousins, and nieces
We won't waste time playing the violin
But can't help longing for what might have been

We can't go forward and can't go back
We seem stuck on a dead end track
As we sit and ponder our fate
Both old and new love sure is great

A chance at a new life we now perceive
And miracles happen that we believe
Thus we nourish our ancient dream
Love and hope is our eternal theme

At The Airport

I knew she was a little cutie
As she came closer I had to stare
I had never seen such grace and beauty
All the right curves were certainly there

Quick steps brought her straight to me
The crowd on the concourse seemed to fade
We hugged and kissed where all could see
It's my heaven in the arms of this little maid

Then slowly I set her carry-on down
And greeted her husband with a firm hand shake
They were my guests in my hometown
The duties of a host I could not forsake

It's a difficult act to be nonchalant
With such strong feelings and not let it show
Always pretending to be the gallant
What she and I knew, no others must know

Reality

Looking out upon the world I see reality
Or is it really reality that I see
I suspect what's real may only be inside of me
The things I see and touch are as expected to be

Physical objects have no attributes though
Until an observer's consciousness makes it so
The burning question we would like to know
Can observation create reality from nothing down below?

There is no "deep reality" according to Bohr
It's the quantum description that realists abhor
If we take a quantum leap clear out the door
We may find matter is an illusion, nothing more

Half A Mind

CRACK! The thunder just split the air
It jerked me back with a flash and a flare
So suddenly that it left part of my mind
Dangling unattached by your side or behind

If you sense someone just touched your hair
It is my essence stranded in your care
If you see a shadow from the corner of your eye
You'll know it's me always close by

Now you'll have no privacy and that's a rub
I'll be with you whether you're sleeping or in the tub
Now you know you will never be alone
But protected by the love we have known

As for the rest of me, it's now clear
Absent-minded means only partly here
But with half a mind, I'll do just dandy
While the other half cavorts in Sandy

Rrring!

"Hello", she said, with a voice quite low
As she answered the phone from her bed
Then she quickly arose to go below
"Hold on darlin", she said

Love aroused this comely lass
From a nest all comfy and warm
For a chance she could not pass
To meet her lover in any form

Down in a room all her own
It's where she works all day
It's where she goes to be alone
It's really her private "get away"

In private they talked and laughed
Trivial stuff is all that was said
Anyone listening would have thought them daft
With a big happy smile, she went back to bed

Somedays

Somedays I miss you so much
Somedays your almost here
I can feel your spirit right beside me
My minds eye can see you so clear

Somedays I have a conversation
When others only see an empty chair
Somedays I reach out to hug you
Then find my arms just holding air

You may think that I'm just lonely
Or perhaps my cogs have slipped a gear
I'm so in love with you only
And live for the time when you'll be here

Plagued By A Dragon

I'm plagued by that old dragon again
I know the great treasures that lie ahead
I want to claim them so much I'm in pain
But Wait has confounded my head

He says the pleasure is in the anticipation
But I sure think enough is enough
When she says "I'm all yours," in expectation
Prolonged waiting sure is tough

Wait doesn't know what it's all about
To be at the edge of lush pasture
After many long years of drought
To be within only one step to rapture

Still Wait says I must do without
I know he's in charge of waiting
I'd like to clobber him on the snout
And start right now with our dating

The Boss

This small token makes me feel good
No need for thanks, it's all understood
I like having my way you see
So I propose this for you and me
I'll decide the big things, you decide the small
And if we don't know where a decision should fall
You have the job of sorting them all
This seems to me as being pretty fair
With no decisions left hanging in the air
It's certainly better than a coin toss
That way we agree that I'm the boss

Ah Sunup

As the sun rose over yonder mountain
She breathed in deeply the fresh morning air
I saw her looking out over our valley
Although I was watching, she was unaware

I can see the beauty in all of nature
But none so fair as her perfection
With the sun highlighting her shapely form
Then sparkling blue eyes turned in my direction

Instantly her pretty smile flashed
A welcome that warmed my soul
A welcome that expressed her love
As we came together to make a whole

Guard Those Thoughts

I sit at my kitchen table
Thoughts meandering through former times
Fighting melancholy as best I'm able
Listening to those lonesome wind chimes

As the hours wear on toward the end of day
And shadows lengthen in the autumn sun
Those tinkling sounds sure seem to say
You're alone pal, the count down has begun

Then rising to more rational thought
Yes, I'm alone but I'm far from done
I'll take down those chimes as I know I ought
And guard each thought one by one

So many opportunities lie ahead
So many mountains I must scale
My girl is waiting to be wed
With her beside me, I cannot fail

Behind The Hippocampus

The hippocampus at the front of the brain
May be the area where memories reign
Recollection is a very subtle function
Sometimes we get sidetracked at the junction

Sometimes our memories are vividly clear
Complete scenarios can instantly appear
Sometimes training and practice help for awhile
There is no certainty like just opening a file

Behind the hippocampus it's all sort of new
We suspect when activated there is deja vu
It's a feeling that you've seen it or been there before
It may be a feeling or maybe there is more

The Aura

There is a strange emanation
I feel whenever she's near
Like a subtle ethereal vibration
That kicks my hormones in high gear

Strange is the power of her aura
I sense it at least 50 feet away
It charges my emotions with a plethora
Of feelings that sure make my day

If you think that I act distracted
That I don't pay attention to what you say
It may be that I have just reacted
That my reason has been plucked away

I Look To The East

Each day when I look to the east and stare
Far beyond yonder mountains I'm acutely aware
True love awaits me far far away over there
I'm tempted to commence my trek eastward I swear

Thus far the bonds of reason still hold
It would be sheer folly to arrive unannounced I'm told
But I could easily do it; I'm just that bold
The treasures and pleasures there waiting are better than gold

If one day I should turn up gone
You can be sure reason lost, I left at dawn
Any report that I'm missing should be withdrawn
I'll be headed eastward; something is urging me on

The Great Spirit

The Great Spirit has dealt our hand
And we are committed to stay in the game
Tho we know not what the Great Spirit planned
We marvel how he made us so much the same

The Great Spirit taught the grizzly how to fish
And the eagle to spot its prey from high above
He made the moon and stars so we can wish
He also made Ruth and Virg so they can love

The Great Spirit is sure in his grand design
And never overlooks any small detail
When the paths of our lives come into line,
We'll know the Great Spirit has prepared the trail

He has said to the wolf and the owl
Watch over these two they are my pride
So in a cold winters night we hear the wolf howl
We'll be warm and cozy lying side by side

And when the wise old owl says "who who"
It's the Great Spirit watching through his eyes
We know we'll be protected whatever we do
For love is the strongest of all possible ties

Love

Love is a language of delightful sensations
Far more eloquent than words
It's the medium which gives us communications
With the spiritual

Loves expression is intelligible to the heart
As it touches the most sublime passions
And elevates us to tenderness and joy and sets us apart
From barbarous and discordant fashions

Love inspires the contemplative mind to examine relations
And read the wisdom, strength and beauty of God above
Love breaths to the ear the clearest intimations
How nobly eloquent of Deity is my woman's love

There Is Magic

If I but had a silver tongue
And a magic way with words
I'd tell of life when we were young
When we thought a lot of the bees and birds

I'd also tell of a lifetime lost
Of three generations taken away
We'll never know what was our cost
Life goes on though old and gray

I'd tell how we have a greater respect
For precious moments set aside in time
What is past we cannot collect
But we still have a magic mountain to climb

I know there's magic in them thar slopes
With precious gems hidden along the trail
Buoyed by our dreams and hopes
We'll continue to search for the Holy Grail

By The River

My heart was aquiver as she sat by the river
The water was so inviting
When she arose and took off her clothes
I found it quite exciting
I was thinking of sin as she beckoned me in
The water was so inviting
What seemed the oddest, I used to be modest
I found it quite exciting
The weather not cold and she being bold
The water was so inviting
Her nipples stood out so without a doubt
I found it quite exciting
Then I awoke just as she spoke
My dream was so inviting
To think of her there with no pubic hair
I found it quite exciting

An Angels Voice

I just heard a voice; it came in loud and clear
As though an angel on my shoulder was speaking in my ear
She said do not despair, I shall have my wish
She knows the one I love is a real choice dish

I ask about the future, please tell me of the time
She said that I will know it; it'll come to me in rhyme
She said of all the forces God has in his hand
Love is by far the strongest and everything is planned

It may be best to wonder, not knowing of my fate
But with her assurance, I know that I can wait
I said that I was worried about our allotted years
Would they be long or short? She said belay your fears

Although I always wonder and can't wait to see
If it comes in rhyme, what year rhymes with see
My angel would not tell me more
Of course there is a year that rhymes with more

Only One Thing On My Mind

I feel the urge to write my dear
But my mind has drawn a blank
If judged by rhyme or wit, I'd be in the rear
Girls all love a winner so don't look at how I rank

I want to say how much I love you
But it has all been said before
Days and nights without you sure do make me blue
I long to hug and kiss you and invite you in my door

I wish I could have you always by my side
You would be my partner in everything we do
Life's great adventure would be a joyous ride
Please wait for me darling so we can start anew

Number One

Many years have come and gone
But I'm still number one she tells me
Many children all raised and gone
But I'm still number one she tells me
Many things I dare not think about
But I'm still number one she tells me
Many trials and heart aches she's worked out
But I'm still number one she tells me
Many joyful times with family and alone
But I'm still number one she tells me
Many hours spent talking on the phone
But I'm still number one she tells me
Many dreams have not yet come to pass
But I'm still number one she tells me
Many times I've sighed and cried alas
But I'm still number one she tells me

Glowing Thoughts

When the suns last rays gild the mountain tops
I wrap warm thoughts of you about me and lie down to pleasant
dreams
Comforted by our love so strong and real
When the suns first rays gild the mountain tops
I arise with thoughts of you caressing me like a robe
Thoughts of you are with me in the shower
And with me at breakfast and at work
As I gaze upon all the beauty that nature made
And contemplate the intricacies of life
I know for sure God created thee for me to love
Thinking of you, I'm sure that I must glow in the dark

A Tortured Mind

The stark white walls meet at the corner
I understand how my space is tiny
And the walls are padded and soft
The lock on the door is bright and shiny
But I've got a secret that I carefully guard
I never let on when they come to see me
I've been practicing and thinking hard
By concentrating I really can see
The fourth dimension where the corner meets the floor
And though it really tires my mind to try
I see one wall move just a little, sometimes more
Leaving a small opening there that I spy
Now I must work on getting small like a mole
And not let them see me getting so wee
Then one day I'll squeeze through that hole
I'll be out, I'll be gone, I'll be free

Wherever You May Be

Once you've lived in Nevada
It'll always be your home
You may surely wish you had a
Stayed and never left to roam

Nevada has everything that's best
Sage covered mountains and wide valleys
A true symbol of the west
That sure beats city streets and alleys

Its people live and love with a passion
They have a real zest for living
Hard work and honesty is their fashion
Every day in every way it's thanksgiving

Whether you're in Buenos Aries or Granada
New York City or Paris or even Rome
Once you've lived in Nevada
You can always call it home

The Canyon Wall

My memory is like a canyon
That has worn a channel through my mind
The story of my life is told
In Braille on those canyon walls in bold

There's a well used trail winding down
From the rim down into the depths
There are places on that wall I love so much
Places worn smooth and polished from my touch

Farther down some memories are too dim
I often can't retrieve many of them
Way way down there's a spot denoting a loss
On this spot I've set a small white cross

Each time I go down that way
I lay a fresh red rose as if to say
This is a very special memory for me
But memory is all it can ever be

The Dance

Pure and primitive our need to dance
If you've danced alone, you know what it can be
Close your eyes and let your movements enhance
The rhythm of nature that come so naturally

The artist sees the pure beauty in motion
The dancer feels this beauty and grace
He gives it form like waves in the ocean
Merging with nature in a flowing embrace

Dancing with a partner gives a special feeling
Two bodies moving together as if one
That's why romantics find it so appealing
It promotes closeness and it's fun

Three Little Words

I wish I could shout from the highest mountain
What I dare only whisper to myself
If only I could sound a loud trumpet
And send my message through out the land
It's all said in three little words of magic
That have made my life so dramatic
I want others to know my good fortune
So they can say, "Oh, how lucky is he"
If you haven't guessed what those words are
They are simply "SHE LOVES ME'

The Moving Line

I've seen the future
And I've lived the past
It's a mighty fine line
That divides and moving fast
Looking ahead it's very bright
With a few clouds drifting by
Looking back is a shining light
That fades into the distant past
I've hitched my belt to that moving line
If I stumble, I'll still go along
Hoping to stay in the bright sunshine
There is no stopping even if I would
It's a one way ticket some may say
I love the trip and the view is good

Confidence

Do not live your life in fear
That what you have may disappear
Take joy that you are you
Have confidence what you can do
Life's only certainty I proclaim
You only achieve where you aim
Of course you will not achieve
If you fail to aim; fail to believe
You cannot risk it if you have it not
You cannot lose what you haven't got
What you have is always at risk
Tomorrow it could be gone in a whisk
Besting a challenge is part of the fun
Starting over is a pretty big one

Duty

Duty is with us always
As imperative as destiny
Duty rises with us in the morning
And sits by our pillow at night
It" s with us in prosperity and adversity
Unavoidable as any necessity
Avoiding the straight highway of duty
Leads directly to the labyrinth of error

My Prayer

Her lips give such a promise
As they are eagerly touching mine
Lord knows we've waited a lifetime
And if we've earned any credits
Please let us draw on them now
Why let the bear taste honey
And never ever have any more
Why give the seedling some water
And then let it die of thirst
Please find a way, Lord
So that I can claim her as mine
With each breath our lives grow shorter
But we still have so much to give
We have tasted and savored each other
I pray we are in your design
I know only the devil would tempt us
Teasing with what could have been
You know I was once young and stupid
So stupid that I once let her go
Surely so many years of waiting
Can serve as penance in a way
For mistakes I made long ago

Faith Of A Private Man

Vic is a gentle man
Kind in all of his ways
He loves a lady as only he can
He has loved her for 21900 days

She's the choicest catch in all the land
Witty, smart, pretty and cute
But Vic cannot have her hand
Their love has taken a different route

They talk and plan but of course no ring
He knows their wishes can't come true
Hope flows freely from an eternal spring
Is hope all they can ever do?

Hope gives substance to Vic's life
He really does not walk alone
Hoping to someday have a wife
He dreams and plans in a twilight zone

How To Prepare

Strive to rise above the mundane
To seek spiritual and philosophical knowledge
Thus preparing for your final bane
When death tips you over the edge

While here, if truth can indeed be found
Agile thinkers may well be the key
Cast not your lot on unfertile ground
Better to ponder the things you cannot see

Remember, he who sows may not reap
Except for satisfaction and esteem
Be glad you have duties you must keep
A job well done should be your dream

This Thing Called Love

Total,overwhelming,absolute, and complete
To know you have this kind of love
From another human is more than neat
With no reservation, it ranks above
Any happiness that man can conceive
When all 5 senses completely agree
You must give this love in order to receive
There's more than our senses tell, I guarantee
There is an inner something that makes us swell
With a warm bubbling over, hard to describe
A sense of well being we know so well
A real intoxication when you're able to imbibe

The West Wind

The message you sent
Arrived on the west wind
I immediately knew what it meant
What a wonderful way to send
As the wind caressed my cheek
And ruffled my hair like your hand
I felt your heart speak
Direct to my heart as planned
The tender moments we share
As together we dream
Only shows how much we care
Yes, we are the dream team
So blow me your kisses on any breeze
The thoughts of love they convey
Warms my heart with such ease
It's your hugs and kisses in a beautiful bouquet

Big Mystery

Female humans like a cat
Man cannot impose his will
So nice to caress when in the mood
They pick the time and place
Very mysterious how they think
No rules of logic cluttered there
Assumptions one should never make
As many poor lad has come to know
Even the wisest knows not why
We let them have control

If Only

She held me in her hand
So private and tender with care
Her eyes looked into mine and we knew
Knew what we wanted so much
No words between us were spoken
Tho I sighed and thrilled at her touch
Our breathing grew heavy as we
Couldn't help looking down to see
Certain changes were happening to us
Her breath was hot and sweet as we kissed
Yes, we knew what we wanted so much
Then the phone rang at five after six
I awoke with a start to hear
Her voice husky and low and so dear

Out West

Out west is the place
Where people go to start over
A place if you want to start a new race
Where your life can be in tall clover
If your life now is searching for zest
It may be time for a jump-start
For a real zest for living, go west
Don't try to analyze or take it apart
West has to be north of yucca
For best results as everyone knows
It also must be west of Winnemucca
West of Winnemucca where the wild wind blows
Strange why this area is so critical
Because that's where conservatives reside
Some might think it to be political
Just pick a cowboy to be your guide

Just Suppose

Do you suppose that it could be
That in another time we were wed
That could be the answer, don't you see
If there was another life we once led

Do you suppose you were once my bride
In some far off time and place
That we shared a life of joy and pride
That life now gone without a trace

There is something inside us that seems to say
We belong! We belong! We belong!
Could an old memory surface this way
Could it really be this strong

Do you suppose we were lovers by design
Powerless to control our fate
That I've always liked yours and you've always liked mine
No wonder our love has always been great

A Letter To Ruth

Darling, in case you can't read my mind
Here are some things that you should know
I believe our very souls are now entwined
As my love for you continues to grow

I cherish memories of a long gone past
Memories of when we were in our prime
Sadly, I can't forget the last
Six decades that should have been our time

Now you've given me so much to live for
So many things that we plan to do
There is a bright new world we have in store
Please wait for me. I'll wait for you

And as we wait, we' re not growing older
Our bubble in time has come to rest
Come lay your head upon my shoulder
We both know how much we are blest

    Love, virg

Wild Fire

You've awakened a raging beast
Within my breast is a fire
No taming it for now at least
'Till I've achieved my hearts desire

I cannot sleep nor can I eat
My love is charging wild
My dreams are so hot and sweet
I'm as naive as any child

If you would sooth my aching plight
And save my heart from ravage
Please kiss me, dear, and hold me tight
To appease the raging savage

The Date

She took the train to Lander street
To meet her lover there
Undeterred by rain nor snow nor sleet
Her striking beauty caused everyone to stare

He was waiting for her to step down
And admired the bright yellow dress she wore
They agreed to meet in this small town
To stay what gossips would deplore

He helped her into his waiting carriage
And off into the night they sped
These lovers had it all except a marriage
Alas she was already wed

They dined alone with fine wine
Touching and talking til the hour was late
Time sped quickly til well after nine
Twas the only time they ever had a date

Brilliant Is Cool

Being brilliant is a skill
It's called thinking out of the box
It can be learned, if you will
Isn't it intuition that guides the fox

Instinct is often better than analysis
When there are tough decisions we must make
Weighing options can lead to paralysis
Listen to your instinct, for heaven sake

How do you learn brilliance, you may ask
Simply get out of your own way
Then practice, practice, practice as in any task
Practice listening to what your guts have to say

Come Teach Me

Yes, we learn from hard knocks
But it's better to learn from a soft touch
Why lasting scars and painful shocks
When the gentle caress of a soft hand says so much

To touch and be touched with caring
Teaches us value in not being alone
It conveys the knowledge and pleasure of sharing
Experience and hard knocks are overblown

So come, if you will, and teach me
I yearn to know all your ways
You have a special way to reach me
So special far beyond my meager praise

To My Girl

I will lead you in paths you have not known
And I will make darkness light before you
I will watch over you and always be by your side
I will enjoy you and my love will be your shelter
Though our steps through life have traced an intricate design
Now they are footprints side by side in the sands of time
Two sets of prints one large, one small into eternity
Yes, I will show you the heights of utmost passion
And the blissful joy of a warm cuddling nest
I will share with you the joy of being a proud partner
And give you the pride of knowing you are my choice

The Choicest Peach

She spoke in a tongue that was olden
And she mentioned old names that I knew
Her voice was rich, young and golden
How could this old lady be true?

Far far back in time she took me
She had an impish look in her eyes
She captured my heart so completely
I knew I had won the grand prize

But the ways of the devil can be devious
If he gives you your way you must pay
I almost had her in a life previous
Just a taste, then he snatched her away

Now I can see her so tempting and near
Why so high on the tree is the choicest peach?
I'm stretching and reaching without fear
But try as I may, she's still out of reach

Bon Voyage

He stood by her side on the rolling deck
As they watched in awe the receding shore
They had escaped all earthly shackles, by heck
And awaited what adventures lay in store

Family and friends had said their goodbyes
It was bitter sweet to be free at last
Was it the salt air that blurred their eyes
When time is short, can you enjoy it fast

It was a new experience for these two
A little unsteady now in their senior years
With eyes for each other instead of the view
Together they were sailing to new frontiers

Before Daylight

As I look to the east at mornings haze
A pale light in the eastern sky
I'm looking all the way back to former days
When we saddled up before first light

'bout the only sound was creaking leather as we mounted up
The men were quiet, not much talk
Each keeping his own thoughts since the last coffee cup
Then a flash of light and the horses all jump
Someone struck a match to light his bull Durham
Nothing glamorous, just a lot of hard work
It'll be a long day out there in the sun
There is camaraderie here though it's not spoken
It's come along boys lets get the job done

The Seeker

To the man who is always yearning to know
Who asks "Who am I" and "Why am I here"
You've joined the universal search; a desire to grow
When will life's deeper meaning appear?

These timeless questions plague people around the world
There is much to learn from those who've gone before
The time for thinkers has come; ah liberty unfurled
Great discoveries lie ahead if we would but explore

There are a host of benefits in this beautiful life
More substantial things than security and success
Seek the truth and forget the daily strife
The joy of loving is a never-ending process

A Cute Little Package

I can't put into words all that I desire
I know what it is; I've known it since my youth
There's a bundle of many things that I admire
Wrapped in a cute little package called Ruth

Just to hear her voice sets my heart on fire
God has given her everything she needs
There is nothing else that I require
I wonder where my strong desire leads

Beauty and compassion and she loves me
But there is a barrier we cannot cross
It sure seems we have a destiny
But once before she was my loss

When It's Forty Below

I'm not afraid of the winter storm
Because I've learned how to keep me warm
When the north wind blows with sleet and snow
My thoughts hasten to a girl I know

Tho I'm nearly froze and my hands are numb
I see her handing me a hot buttered rum
She looks so darling in her fluffy white robe
If I ask, she'd probably disrobe

Even if it gets to forty below
Inside I'll be warm and all aglow
Knowing my girl this time will wait
There will be no one else even if I'm late

My Office

If these walls could speak and tell
What a story there would be
If these office walls I know so well
Could recount all the things they see

It would be startling to quite a few
Who never thought of us this way
They really would be shocked if they knew
What this old desk could have to say

Covered with papers, my work is my excuse
Contracts and records that I must keep
Only you and I know it has had a different use
Ah, the memories that I can reap

As I sit here and contemplate
I can see you just before me
I savor what has been on my plate
Please come again I implore thee

On Top Of The World

Feeling young and walking tall
That's why I strut and click my heels
I'm loving life and having a ball
I wish I could tell you how good it feels

It's because of the future I expect
Love and excitement are coming my way
Anticipation has a tremendous effect
I eagerly appreciate each dawning day

Knowing I am loved without restraint
There is no mountain I cannot scale
I have no regrets nor any complaint
No matter the challenge, I shall prevail

My woman's love has given me strength
Has brightened and energized my soul
Even tho we taste of love at arms length
I know one day we will achieve our goal

Friends

Who are the gardeners that make our souls bloom
Who are the beauticians that make us radiant and smile
Who are they who are happy when we enter a room
Who are they that give us strength to go the extra mile

They are the ones whose company we enjoy
They are the ones who we like to be near
They are the ones we know as the real McCoy
They are all the friends that we love and hold dear

Imagination I

My mind always caresses her prow to stern
Every small detail I wish to learn
Certain anatomical twinges I begin to feel
As my mind comes to rest upon her keel

The power to imagine is my greatest gift
With wind in the sails, I let it drift
I can imagine so many implausible scenes
Like slipping my hand into her jeans

Or if my approach so far has bombed
If the sea is quiet and we are becalmed
She may say to me," do we dare
Explore each other, look and compare"

Sometimes my mind with nary a falter
Has seen us hand in hand before the alter
There has been the house with white picket fence
Always, of course, in some future tense

Imagination is such an unstable thing
From many extremes it's prone to swing
But when coupled with hopes and dreams
It may be a window to the future it seems

Imagination II

Imagination is the crux of all
The salesman imagines before he makes a call
The builder imagines before he constructs
The teacher must imagine before she instructs

That picture that appears in ones mind
Is the attribute that distinguishes mankind
Even the artist must imagine before he draws
And the actor imagines what will bring applause

The architect imagines the building before he designs
The ceo and politician imagines his course before he resigns
Before any positive step can be taken
Ones imagination must first awaken

Even lovers imagine as they proceed
Imagining their actions and what they'll need
Yes, imagination is such a powerful thing
The more you have, the more it will bring

So imagine the future, as you want it to be
Never stop imagining; actually it's free
A good imagination accompanied with a nudge
And things start happening; you be the judge

The Enigma Of Succes

Twilight can last a long long time
Age after age has rolled on by
We now wander in the twilight of our prime
How beautiful the sunset in our sky

We have been delivered and evolved
From one life well lived to the next
The enigma of success we have solved
As we soar ever higher without pretext

We are no stronger or smarter than the rest
We have no advantage or better luck
One thing we have that serves us best
A strong desire to succeed, to rise above the muck

Although we are not the swiftest in the race
There is more to winning than being fast
We have faith and know that we will place
Our success comes since we can wait and last

A Second Chance

Love letters can mean so much
No matter what they say
It's a way for lovers to keep in touch
Affirming their feelings along the way

There is tragedy there I hope to tell
When those letters go astray
Painful worrying that all is not well
That grows worse day by day

After months and years from afar
Those damaged hearts may cease to bleed
Healing in a way with an enormous scar
Damaged lives still have their need

Six decades later would you believe
Those purloined letters were never read
But love has found a way to retrieve
Old emotions long thought dead

Destroying those letters was an evil choice
With ramifications that changed the world
Now those old lovers do rejoice
Hoping for a second chance to be unfurled

Guess What

Should every poetic endeavor
Have a story to tell
Or should it be more clever
And leave you wondering, what the hell

Who cares what the poet thinks
Who cares about his emotion
Or if his ship sails or sinks
As he embarks upon the ocean

Getting A Fix By Phone

Her voice strokes my psyche
Like rubbing silk against my cheek
Caressing, soothing, and exciting me
All one and at the same time

It's familiar, kinda low and sexy
With a timbre all its own
It makes me want to hug and kiss her
Even tho it comes to me by phone

I know her love for me is real
That I value more than life
She sets the smile upon my face
And controls the rhythm of my heart.

Our Secret

There is a monument to me I know
In the heart of a beautiful woman
No higher honor can mortal bestow
She has built it slowly over the years
Lovingly adding piece by piece
The world only sees as it appears
Old friends connected by a long ago past
But I know that as long as there is life
We've merged in body and soul to the last
We are a part of each other as we belong
I toast to the day when our secret life
Will be celebrated with feast and song

A Loss For Words

Here I sit at my old typewriter
Pecking away at the keys
Hoping for a verse that is lighter
That will tickle you down to your knees

But when I read what is written
I'm usually quite surprised too
Sometimes it's not even fitten
To send to a girl like you

If I say you're awfully cute
You may think I'm just kidden
But my taste you really suit
Why is our love forbidden

Winning The Battle

The sharpest weapon in any battle
Is the kind and gentle spirit
However do not succumb to the ills of apathy
For complacency has never led a charge

Indifference is the way of the sloth
Passion and fervor are triumphs companions
He who lightens the burdens of another
Is the victor in worths struggle

Johnstun

Johnstun was her name
Always special in any crowd
The choicest morsel was to be her fame
Just to know her; you felt so proud

Beautiful and honest never coy
Entering a room , she made it glow
With love and warmth and joy
Lucky the man destined to be her beau

Time has enhanced her beauty and grace
Loved by all who've come to know
She's so much more than a pretty face
Lucky the man destined to be her beau

God was pleased when he made this girl
Brimming with love that she does bestow
In any crown, she's the choicest pearl
Lucky the man destined to be her beau

Christmas Time

Each time I admire a yule time tree
With its bells and baubles bright
I think of my girl who waits for me
With multiple charms shinning in a different light

Adorned with a beauty that pleases my eye
Enthusiasm for life that gladdens my heart
A cute little body slender and spry
And feelings about sex that sets her apart

She has a smile that flashes always sincere
And compassion for others wherever they be
She's my partner on a new frontier
My wish for Christmas is her on my knee

The Addict

Whether I'm in the city or somewhere in the sticks
I never feel so much alone
If I have my trusty telephone
And know I can get my hourly fix

I know I shouldn't call you so very very much
Morning noon and night each and every day
Just to hear your voice, maybe nothing new to say
I have a really bad addiction and darling you are my crutch

Sometimes nothing else matters, I just need my high
When I start getting nervous, I know I need to call
After the highest high, then I start to fall
I keep watching the time as the hours pass slowly by